Spanish Verb Conjugation: A Hands-On Guide to the 7 Simple Tenses

WRITTEN BY
Brian Ford

LULU PUBLISHING COMPANY
Morrisville, North Carolina

ISBN 978-1-4357-0420-6

This book is dedicated to those who were always there for me in good times and bad, to those who always believed in me, to those who encouraged me, to those who made me who I am today, my family.

TABLE OF CONTENTS

INSTRUCTIONAL BOOKLET

CONJUGATION BOARDS

THE VERB *HABLAR*

THE VERB *COMER*

THE VERB *VIVIR*

THE NEW LOOK OF SPANISH VERB CONJUGATION

My name is Brian Ford and I have been teaching Spanish for nine years. I am also the District Spanish Coordinator for my school system. I enjoy teaching Spanish, and I am constantly looking for new and innovative ways to teach age-old concepts. When I first began teaching, I noticed that many students in my classes were having trouble with verb conjugation. I repeatedly found myself with the dilemma of needing a more simplified method to effectively teach this concept to my students. Therefore, I began to experiment with several different methods during my early years of teaching. I continued to refine my model of simple verb conjugation, and now I am proud to introduce *Spanish Verb Conjugation: A Hands-On Guide to the 7 Simple Tenses.*

I have used this hands-on method in my classroom for several years and my students have discovered a whole new perspective on verb conjugation and have enjoyed great success. Students relate well to this method by quickly making connections to the Spanish concepts through the use of the English language thus increasing retention and building confidence. Over the years, I have noticed a marked improvement in students' reading comprehension, writing, and speaking ability. Test scores have risen dramatically and students have developed more confidence in expressing themselves through Spanish conversation and composition. Now, 28 individual state championships and 70 individual regional championships later in World Language competition, my students are looked upon as one of the top scoring high schools in Spanish language in the state.

Instead of conjugation being a dull and boring drill that involves writing page after page of monotonous verb conjugations, students now have a unique, hands-on approach that allows them to actively learn the subject pronouns, verb stems, verb endings, conjugations, and usage of regular simple tense verbs. This hybrid instructional book / hands-on learning kit will change your perspective on conjugation and you will never look at Spanish verbs the same way again!

WHAT IS INCLUDED IN THIS BOOK?

The instructional section of this book contains each of the following topics with English examples that help students to make connections to the Spanish concepts thus increasing retention, building confidence, and improving speaking, reading comprehension, and writing, all in one page or less:

- Conjugation
- Subject Pronouns
- The Infinitive Form of the Verb
- The Stem and Ending of the Verb
- The Uses and Conjugations of the Present Tense
- The Uses and Conjugations of the Imperfect Tense
- The Uses and Conjugations of the Preterit Tense
- The Uses and Conjugations of the Future Tense
- The Uses and Conjugations of the Conditional Tense
- The Uses and Conjugations of the Present Subjunctive
- The Uses and Conjugations of the Imperfect Subjunctive
- Common Verbs Conjugated Like *Hablar*, *Comer*, & *Vivir*

The hands-on learning kit contains the following:

- (7) Simple Tense Usage Boards
- (7) Simple Tense Usage Card Sets

- (3) (-ar, -er, -ir) Present Tense Conjugation Boards
- (3) (-ar, -er, -ir) Imperfect Tense Conjugation Boards
- (3) (-ar, -er, -ir) Preterit Tense Conjugation Boards
- (3) (-ar, -er, -ir) Future Tense Conjugation Boards
- (3) (-ar, -er, -ir) Conditional Tense Conjugation Boards
- (3) (-ar, -er, -ir) Present Subjunctive Conjugation Boards
- (3) (-ar, -er, -ir) Imperfect Subjunctive Conjugation Boards

- (3) Subject Pronoun Card Sets
- (3) Verb Stem Card Sets (Hablar, Comer, & Vivir)
- (3) Verb Endings Card Sets (Regular –ar, -er, & -ir)
- (3) Translation Card Sets (Hablar, Comer, & Vivir) in Present Tense – Imperfect Subjunctive

HOW DOES THIS METHOD WORK?

The hands-on kit allows students to apply knowledge they have gained through the instructional portion of this book. The following steps will address the proper use of the hands-on kit:

STEP 1: Begin by reading through the instructional section of this book. Then focus on each simple tense individually, beginning with the PRESENT TENSE. Remove the large PRESENT TENSE USAGE BOARD and cut out the PRESENT TENSE USAGE CARDS. Place the PRESENT TENSE USAGE CARDS in a small plastic bag.

STEP 2: Lay the PRESENT TENSE USAGE BOARD on a table. Pour the bag containing the USAGE CARDS onto the table and begin placing the USAGE CARDS on the PRESENT TENSE USAGE BOARD.

STEP 3: Remove the 3 PRESENT TENSE CONJUGATION BOARDS (1–ar, 1 –er, 1 –ir). Then cut out the PRESENT TENSE SUBJECT PRONOUNS, VERB STEMS, VERB ENDINGS and TRANSLATION CARDS for **hablar, comer,** and **vivir**. Place all the cards in a small plastic bag.

STEP 4: Lay the 3 PRESENT TENSE CONJUGATION BOARDS (1 –ar, 1 –er, and 1 –ir) on a table. Thoroughly mix the bag containing the SUBJECT PRONOUNS, VERB STEMS, VERB ENDINGS and TRANSLATION CARDS for **hablar, comer,** and **vivir** in the PRESENT TENSE. Pour the cards onto the table and begin placing the cards in the correct spaces on the appropriate PRESENT TENSE CONJUGATION BOARDS. After completing both the usage and conjugation activities, check your answers using the instructional portion of this book.

STEP 5: Repeat this process with each of the remaining six simple tenses, one at a time, until mastery of usages and conjugations are achieved. With each new tense you will be adding a new set of USAGE CARDS and SUBJECT PRONOUNS, VERB STEMS, VERB ENDINGS, and TRANSLATIONS CARDS to their respective plastic bags. Remember to always keep the USAGE CARDS together in a separate plastic bag from the other cards. For those teachers reading this book, I find it best to use this method as a beginning class activity for my students. Divide your students into small groups and give them an opportunity to work with this method. Use a stopwatch to check their time. You will be amazed at how quickly they complete and master the usages and conjugations of each tense in the –ar, –er, and –ir forms. Once students have mastered the usages and conjugations of each tense, share with them the other regular –ar, –er, and –ir verbs that they can now conjugate correctly (see page 14). You will be amazed at how this method increases retention, builds student confidence, and improves student performance in speaking, reading comprehension, and writing.

WHAT IS CONJUGATION?

Conjugation *is the creation of derived forms of a verb from its principal parts by inflection (regular alteration according to rules of grammar). Conjugation may be affected by person, number, gender, tense, mood, voice, grammatical aspect, or other language-specific factors.*

In simple terms, conjugation means manipulation of the infinitive *(basic form of the verb)* so that it corresponds to the appropriate subject pronoun *(I, you, he / she, we, you (plural), they)*. Here are the present tense conjugations of the infinitives "**to speak**", "**to eat**", and "**to live**":

to speak	to eat	to live
I speak	*I* eat	*I* live
you speak	*you* eat	*you* live
he / she speaks	*he / she* eats	*he / she* lives
we speak	*we* eat	*we* live
you (plural) speak	*you (plural)* eat	*you (plural)* live
they speak	*they* eat	*they* live

The following are the Spanish present tense conjugations of the infinitives **hablar, comer**, and **vivir**.

hablar	comer	vivir
yo habl*o*	*yo* com*o*	*yo* viv*o*
tú habl*as*	*tú* com*es*	*tú* viv*es*
él / ella habl*a*	*él / ella* com*e*	*él / ella* viv*e*
nosotros habl*amos*	*nosotros* com*emos*	*nosotros* viv*imos*
vosotros habl*áis*	*vosotros* com*éis*	*vosotros* viv*ís*
ellos / ellas habl*an*	*ellos / ellas* com*en*	*ellos / ellas* viv*en*

Many Spanish verbs are completely regular, meaning that they follow a specific pattern of conjugation. In this kit you will learn to conjugate regular **-ar**, **-er**, and **-ir** verbs in all seven simple tenses. Before you can do that, you must memorize the subject pronouns on the following page.

SUBJECT PRONOUNS

A subject pronoun is a pronoun used as a subject of a verb. The following list of words are subject pronouns:

SINGULAR SUBJECT PRONOUNS

yo	=	I
tú	=	you (informal)
él	=	he
ella	=	she
* usted	=	you (formal)

PLURAL SUBJECT PRONOUNS

nosotros	=	we (masculine or mixed group)
nosotras	=	we (feminine group)
vosotros	=	you (plural) (informal) (masculine or mixed group)
vosotras	=	you (plural) (informal) (feminine group)
ellos	=	they (masculine or mixed group)
ellas	=	they (feminine group)
* ustedes	=	you (plural) (formal)

Spanish subject pronouns are both similar to and different from the English subject pronouns. For example there are two ways the English word "you" can be expressed in Spanish:

tú* = *you (informal) Use this form when addressing a friend, co-worker, relative, or child.

usted* = *you (formal) Use this form when you wish to show respect to an individual such as your superior, public official, or someone that you do not know well.

There are also two ways of expressing the English "you all":

vosotros / vosotras* = *you all (informal) This form is only used in Spain. Use this form when addressing friends, co-workers, relatives, or children.

ustedes* = *you all (formal) Use this form when you wish to show respect to individuals such as your superiors, public officials, or individuals that you do not know well.

The Spanish language is more gender specific than the English language. This is quite evident with the following subject pronouns: nosotros / nosotras and ellos / ellas. There are two ways to say "we" and two ways to say "they" in Spanish.

nosotros* = *we (This signifies "we" in the sense of a group containing at least one male.)
nosotras* = *we (This signifies "we" in the sense of a group containing only females.)

vosotros* = *you all (informal) (This signifies "you all" in the sense of a group containing at least one male.)
vosotras* = *you all (informal) (This signifies "you all" in the sense of a group containing only females.)

ellos* = *they (This signifies "they" in the sense of a group containing all males or a mixed group.)
ellas* = *they (This signifies "they" in the sense of a group containing all females.)

*** Usted and ustedes are not included on the subject pronoun cards in this kit.**

THE INFINITIVE FORM OF THE VERB

*The infinitive is the basic form of the verb, such as **to speak, to eat, to live**, etc.* In Spanish, all infinitives end in **-ar**, **-er**, or **-ir**. The **–ar**, **-er**, and **–ir** endings are referred to as the infinitive endings.

EXAMPLES:

-AR VERBS	**-ER VERBS**	**-IR VERBS**
hablar- *to speak*	comer- *to eat*	vivir- *to live*

THE STEM AND ENDING OF A VERB

The verb in Spanish is composed of two parts. The stem and ending. The stem or root of the verb is formed by dropping the infinitive ending (**-ar**, **-er**, or **–ir**).

INFINITIVE	**STEM**
habl**ar**	habl-
com**er**	com-
viv**ir**	viv-

The verb ending will change for each person in the conjugation of regular verbs. In order to conjugate, one must establish to which group a verb belongs. Regular verbs will be divided into three groupings that will be identified by their infinitive endings.

GROUP 1	**GROUP 2**	**GROUP 3**
-ar	**-er**	**-ir**

Each of the three verb groups will have its own unique set of endings for each conjugational tense. It is only necessary to learn the conjugational forms of one sample verb from each grouping in order to be able to conjugate other regular verbs belonging to that grouping. In this kit we will focus on one regular verb from each group: hablar, comer, and vivir.

Now, in order to conjugate a regular verb, follow the steps below:

STEP 1: Correctly identify the verb by its **infinitive ending.**

EXAMPLE: habl**ar** com**er** viv**ir**

STEP 2: Locate the verb stem or root by removing the infinitive ending.

EXAMPLE: habl- com- viv-

STEP 3: Add the appropriate **ending** that corresponds to the *subject pronoun.*

EXAMPLE: *yo* habl**o** *tú* com**es** *él / ella* viv**e**

PRESENT TENSE

THE PRESENT TENSE IS USED TO EXPRESS:

A.) *an action or a state of being at the present time.*
B.) *a habitual action.*
C.) *a general truth, something which is permanently true.*
D.) *vividness when referring to past events.*
E.) *a near future.*
F.) *an action or state of being that occurred in the past and continues up to the present.*

THE PRESENT TENSE IS REGULARY FORMED AS FOLLOWS:

-AR VERBS- Drop the **-ar** ending of the infinitive and add the following endings: **-o, -as, -a, -amos, -áis, -an**

habl**o**	*(I speak)*	habl**amos**	*(We speak)*
habl**as**	*(You speak)*	habl**áis**	*(You (plural) speak)*
habl**a**	*(He / she speaks)*	habl**an**	*(They speak)*

-ER VERBS- Drop the **-er** ending of the infinitive and add the following endings: **-o, -es, -e, -emos, -éis, -en**

com**o**	*(I eat)*	com**emos**	*(We eat)*
com**es**	*(You eat)*	com**éis**	*(You (plural) eat)*
com**e**	*(He / she eats)*	com**en**	*(They eat)*

-IR VERBS- Drop the **-ir** ending of the infinitive and add the following endings: **-o, -es, -e, -imos, -ís, -en**

viv**o**	*(I live)*	viv**imos**	*(We live)*
viv**es**	*(You live)*	viv**ís**	*(You (plural) live)*
viv**e**	*(He / she lives)*	viv**en**	*(They live)*

IMPERFECT TENSE

THE IMPERFECT TENSE IS USED TO EXPRESS:

A.) an action that was going on in the past at the same time as another action.
B.) an action that was going on in the past when another action occurred.
C.) an action that a person did habitually in the past.
D.) a description of a mental, emotional, or physical condition in the past.
E.) the time of day in the past.

F.) an action or state of being that occurred in the past and lasted for a certain length of time prior to another past action.

G.) an indirect quotation in the past.

THE IMPERFECT TENSE IS REGULARY FORMED AS FOLLOWS:

-AR VERBS- Drop the **-ar** ending of the infinitive and add the following endings: **-aba, -abas, -aba, -ábamos, -abais, -aban**

habl**aba**	*(I was speaking)*	habl**ábamos**	*(We were speaking)*
habl**abas**	*(You were speaking)*	habl**abais**	*(You (plural) were speaking)*
habl**aba**	*(He / she was speaking)*	habl**aban**	*(They were speaking)*

-ER VERBS- Drop the **-er** ending of the infinitive and add the following endings: **-ía, -ías, -ía, -íamos, -íais, -ían**

com**ía**	*(I was eating)*	com**íamos**	*(We were eating)*
com**ías**	*(You were eating)*	com**íais**	*(You (plural) were eating)*
com**ía**	*(He / she was eating)*	com**ían**	*(They were eating)*

-IR VERBS- Drop the **-ir** ending of the infinitive and add the following endings: **-ía, -ías, -ía, -íamos, -íais, -ían**

viv**ía**	*(I was living)*	viv**íamos**	*(We were living)*
viv**ías**	*(You were living)*	viv**íais**	*(You (plural) were living)*
viv**ía**	*(He / she was living)*	viv**ían**	*(They were living)*

PRETERIT TENSE

THE PRETERIT TENSE IS USED TO EXPRESS:

A.) an action that was completed at some point in the past.

THE PRETERIT TENSE IS REGULARY FORMED AS FOLLOWS:

-AR VERBS- Drop the **-ar** ending of the infinitive and add the following endings: **-é, -aste, -ó, -amos, -asteis, -aron**

habl**é**	*(I spoke)*	habl**amos**	*(We spoke)*
habl**aste**	*(You spoke)*	habl**asteis**	*(You (plural) spoke)*
habl**ó**	*(He / she spoke)*	habl**aron**	*(They spoke)*

-ER VERBS- Drop the **–er** ending of the infinitive and add the following endings: **-í, -iste, -ió, -imos, -isteis, -ieron**

com**í**	*(I ate)*	com**imos**	*(We ate)*
com**iste**	*(You ate)*	com**isteis**	*(You (plural) ate)*
com**ió**	*(He / she ate)*	com**ieron**	*(They ate)*

-IR VERBS- Drop the **-ir** ending of the infinitive and add the following endings: **-í, -iste, -ió, -imos, -isteis, -ieron**

viv**í**	*(I lived)*	viv**imos**	*(We lived)*
viv**iste**	*(You lived)*	viv**isteis**	*(You (plural) lived)*
viv**ió**	*(He / she lived)*	viv**ieron**	*(They lived)*

FUTURE TENSE

THE FUTURE TENSE IS USED TO EXPRESS:

A.) an action or a state of being that will take place at sometime in the future.
B.) conjecture regarding the present.
C.) probability regarding the present.
D.) an indirect quotation.

THE FUTURE TENSE IS REGULARY FORMED AS FOLLOWS:

-AR, -ER, & -IR VERBS- Add the following endings to the whole infinitive: **-é, -ás, -á, -emos, -éis, -án**

hablar**é**	*(I shall speak)*	hablar**emos**	*(We shall speak)*
hablar**ás**	*(You will speak)*	hablar**éis**	*(You (plural) will speak)*
hablar**á**	*(He / she will speak)*	hablar**án**	*(They will speak)*

comer**é**	*(I shall eat)*	comer**emos**	*(We shall eat)*
comer**ás**	*(You will eat)*	comer**éis**	*(You (plural) will eat)*
comer**á**	*(He / she will eat)*	comer**án**	*(They will eat)*

vivir**é**	*(I shall live)*	vivir**emos**	*(We shall live)*
vivir**ás**	*(You will live)*	vivir**éis**	*(You (plural) will live)*
vivir**á**	*(He / she will live)*	vivir**án**	*(They will live)*

CONDITIONAL TENSE

THE CONDITIONAL TENSE IS USED TO EXPRESS:

A.) an action that one would do if something else were possible.
B.) a conditional desire.
C.) an indirect quotation.
D.) conjecture regarding the past.
E.) probability regarding the past.

THE CONDITIONAL TENSE IS REGULARY FORMED AS FOLLOWS:

-AR, -ER, & -IR VERBS- Add the following endings to the whole infinitive: **-ía, -ías, -ía, íamos, -íais, -ían**

hablar**ía**	*(I would speak)*	hablar**íamos**	*(We would speak)*
hablar**ías**	*(You would speak)*	hablar**íais**	*(You (plural) would speak)*
hablar**ía**	*(He / she would speak)*	hablar**ían**	*(They would speak)*

comer**ía**	*(I would eat)*	comer**íamos**	*(We would eat)*
comer**ías**	*(You would eat)*	comer**íais**	*(You (plural) would eat)*
comer**ía**	*(He / she would eat)*	comer**ían**	*(They would eat)*

vivir**ía**	*(I would live)*	vivir**íamos**	*(We would live)*
vivir**ías**	*(You would live)*	vivir**íais**	*(You (plural) would live)*
vivir**ía**	*(He / she would live)*	vivir**ían**	*(They would live)*

PRESENT SUBJUNCTIVE

THE PRESENT SUBJUNCTIVE IS USED:

A.) in a command in the ***usted*** *or* ***ustedes*** *form, either in the affirmative or negative.*
B.) in a negative command in the familiar form ***(tú)****.*
C.) in a negative command in the second person plural ***(vosotros)****.*
D.) in a command in the first person plural, either in the affirmative or negative ***(nosotros)****.*
E.) after a verb that expresses some kind of wish, insistence, preference, suggestion, or request.
F.) after a verb that expresses doubt, fear, joy, hope, sorrow, or some other emotion.
G.) after certain impersonal expressions that show necessity, doubt, regret, importance, urgency, or possibility.

H.) after certain conjunctions of time, such as, ***antes (de) que, cuando, en cuanto, después (de) que, hasta que, mientras,*** *and the like. The subjunctive form of the verb is used when introduced by any of these time conjunctions if the time referred to is either indefinite or is expected to take place in the future.*

I.) after certain conjunctions that express a condition, negation, purpose, such as, ***a menos que, con tal que, para que, a fin de que, sin que, en caso (de) que,*** *and the like.*

J.) after certain adverbs, such as, ***acaso, quizá,*** *and* ***tal vez****.*
K.) after ***aunque,*** *if the action has not yet occurred.*
L.) in an adjectival clause if the antecedent is something or someone that is indefinite, negative, vague, or nonexistent.
M.) after ***por más que*** *or* ***por mucho que****.*
N.) after the expression ***ojalá (que),*** *which expresses a great desire.*

THE PRESENT SUBJUNCTIVE IS REGULARY FORMED AS FOLLOWS:

-AR VERBS- Drop the **-ar** ending of the infinitive and add the following endings: **-e, -es, -e, -emos, -éis, -en**

habl**e**	*(That I may speak)*	habl**emos**	*(That we may speak)*
habl**es**	*(That you may speak)*	habl**éis**	*(That you (plural) may speak)*
habl**e**	*(That he / she may speak)*	habl**en**	*(That they may speak)*

-ER VERBS- Drop the **-er** ending of the infinitive and add the following endings: **-a, -as, -a, -amos, -áis, -an**

com**a**	*(That I may eat)*	com**amos**	*(That we may eat)*
com**as**	*(That you may eat)*	com**áis**	*(That you (plural) may eat)*
com**a**	*(That he / she may eat)*	com**an**	*(That they may eat)*

-IR VERBS- Drop the **-ir** ending of the infinitive and add the following endings: **-a, -as, -a, -amos, -áis, -an**

viv**a**	*(That I may live)*	viv**amos**	*(That we may live)*
viv**as**	*(That you may live)*	viv**áis**	*(That you (plural) may live)*
viv**a**	*(That he / she may live)*	viv**an**	*(That they may live)*

IMPERFECT SUBJUNCTIVE

NOTES ON THE IMPERFECT SUBJUNCTIVE

A.) This past tense is used for the same reasons as the present subjunctive.
B.) The main difference between the present and imperfect subjunctive is the time of the action.

C.) If the verb in the main clause is in the imperfect, preterit, conditional, or past perfect tense, the imperfect subjunctive is ordinarily used in the dependent clause (if use of the subjunctive is required).

D.) The imperfect subjunctive is used after **como si** *to express a condition contrary to fact.*

THE IMPERFECT SUBJUNCTIVE IS REGULARY FORMED AS FOLLOWS:

-AR VERBS- Drop the **-ar** ending of the infinitive and add the following endings: **-ara, -aras, -ara, -áramos, -arais, -aran**

habl**ara**	*(That I might speak)*	habl**áramos**	*(That we might speak)*
habl**aras**	*(That you might speak)*	habl**arais**	*(That you (plural) might speak)*
habl**ara**	*(That he / she might speak)*	habl**aran**	*(That they might speak)*

-ER VERBS- Drop the **-er** ending of the infinitive and add the following endings: **-iera, -ieras, -iera, -iéramos, -ierais, -ieran**

com**iera**	*(That I might eat)*	com**iéramos**	*(That we might eat)*
com**ieras**	*(That you might eat)*	com**ierais**	*(That you (plural) might eat)*
com**iera**	*(That he / she might eat)*	com**ieran**	*(That they might eat)*

-IR VERBS- Drop the **-ir** ending of the infinitive and add the following endings: **-iera, -ieras, -iera, -iéramos, -ierais, -ieran**

viv**iera**	*(That I might live)*	viv**iéramos**	*(That we might live)*
viv**ieras**	*(That you might live)*	viv**ierais**	*(That you (plural) might live)*
viv**iera**	*(That he / she might live)*	viv**ieran**	*(That they might live)*

COMMON –AR VERBS CONJUGATED LIKE *HABLAR*

alquilar- to rent
ayudar- to help
bailar- to dance
buscar- to look for
caminar- to walk
cantar- to sing
cocinar- to cook
comprar- to buy
contestar- to answer
dejar- to allow
desear- to desire
enseñar- to teach
entrar- to enter
enviar- to send
escuchar- to listen to
esperar- to hope, to wait for
estudiar- to study
firmar- to sign
ganar- to win or earn
gastar- to spend money
lavar- to wash
llegar- to arrive
llevar- to wear, to carry
mandar- to order
mirar- to watch, to look at
necesitar- to need
olvidar- to forget
pagar- to pay for
practicar- to practice
preguntar- to ask (a question)
preparar- to prepare
regresar- to return
saludar- to greet
tocar- to play (an instrument)
tomar- to take or to drink
trabajar- to work
viajar- to travel
visitar- to visit

COMMON –ER VERBS CONJUGATED LIKE *COMER*

aprender- to learn
beber- to drink
comprender- to understand
correr- to run
creer- to believe
deber- to have to, to owe
esconder- to hide
leer- to read
prometer- to promise
romper- to break
temer- to fear
vender- to sell

COMMON –IR VERBS CONJUGATED LIKE *VIVIR*

abrir- to open
admitir- to admit
asistir a- to attend
cubrir- to cover
decidir- to decide
describir- to describe
descubrir- to discover
discutir- to discuss
escribir- to write
existir- to exist
omitir- to omit
partir- to divide
permitir- to permit
recibir- to receive
subir- to climb
sufrir- to suffer
unir- to unite

THE PRESENT TENSE IS USED TO EXPRESS:

A.) ______________________________

B.) ______________________________

C.) ______________________________

D.) ______________________________

E.) ______________________________

F.) ______________________________

THIS PAGE IS INTENTIONALLY BLANK.

THE IMPERFECT TENSE IS USED TO EXPRESS:

A.) ____________________

B.) ____________________

C.) ____________________

D.) ____________________

E.) ____________________

F.) ____________________

G.) ____________________

THIS PAGE IS INTENTIONALLY BLANK.

THE PRETERIT TENSE IS USED TO EXPRESS:

A.) ____

THIS PAGE IS INTENTIONALLY BLANK.

THE FUTURE TENSE IS USED TO EXPRESS:

A.) ____________________

B.) ____________________

C.) ____________________

D.) ____________________

THIS PAGE IS INTENTIONALLY BLANK.

THE CONDITIONAL TENSE

IS USED TO EXPRESS:

A.) ____

B.) ____

C.) ____

D.) ____

E.) ____

THIS PAGE IS INTENTIONALLY BLANK.

THE PRESENT SUBJUNCTIVE IS USED:

A.) ______________________________

B.) ______________________________

C.) ______________________________

D.) ______________________________

E.) ______________________________

F.) ______________________________

G.) ______________________________

H.) ______________________________

I.) ______________________________

J.) ______________________________

K.) ______________________________

L.) ______________________________

M.) ______________________________

N.) ______________________________

THIS PAGE IS INTENTIONALLY BLANK.

NOTES ON THE IMPERFECT SUBJUNCTIVE

A.) ____________________

B.) ____________________

C.) ____________________

D.) ____________________

THIS PAGE IS INTENTIONALLY BLANK.

PRESENT TENSE USAGE CARDS

A.) an action or a state of being at the present time.

B.) a habitual action.

C.) a general truth, something which is permanently true.

D.) vividness when referring to past events.

E.) a near future.

F.) an action or state of being that occurred in the past and continues up to the present.

THIS PAGE IS INTENTIONALLY BLANK.

IMPERFECT TENSE USAGE CARDS

A.) an action that was going on in the past at the same time as another action.

B.) an action that was going on in the past when another action occurred.

C.) an action that a person did habitually in the past.

D.) a description of a mental, emotional, or physical condition in the past.

E.) the time of day in the past.

F.) an action or state of being that occurred in the past and lasted for a certain length of time prior to another past action.

G.) an indirect quotation in the past.

THIS PAGE IS INTENTIONALLY BLANK.

PRETERIT TENSE USAGE CARDS

A.) an action that was completed at some point in the past.

THIS PAGE IS INTENTIONALLY BLANK.

FUTURE TENSE USAGE CARDS

A.) an action or a state of being that will take place at sometime in the future.
B.) conjecture regarding the present.
C.) probability regarding the present.
D.) an indirect quotation.

THIS PAGE IS INTENTIONALLY BLANK.

CONDITIONAL TENSE USAGE CARDS

A.) an action that one would do if something else were possible.

B.) a conditional desire.

C.) an indirect quotation.

D.) conjecture regarding the past.

E.) probability regarding the past.

THIS PAGE IS INTENTIONALLY BLANK.

PRESENT SUBJUNCTIVE USAGE CARDS

A.) in a command in the **usted** *or* **ustedes** *form, either in the affirmative or negative.*

B.) in a negative command in the familiar form **(tú)**.

C.) in a negative command in the second person plural **(vosotros)**.

D.) in a command in the first person plural, either in the affirmative or negative **(nosotros)**.

E.) after a verb that expresses some kind of wish, insistence, preference, suggestion, or request.

F.) after a verb that expresses doubt, fear, joy, hope, sorrow, or some other emotion.

G.) after certain impersonal expressions that show necessity, doubt, regret, importance, urgency, or possibility.

H.) after certain conjunctions of time, such as. **antes (de) que, cuando, en cuanto, después (de) que, hasta que, mientras,** *and the like. The subjunctive form of the verb is used when introduced by any of these time conjunctions if the time referred to is either indefinite or is expected to take place in the future.*

I.) after certain conjunctions that express a condition, negation, purpose, such as, **a menos que, con tal que, para que, a fin de que, sin que, en caso (de) que,** *and the like.*

J.) after certain adverbs, such as, **acaso, quizá**, *and* **tal vez**.

K.) after **aunque,** *if the action has not yet occurred.*

L.) in an adjectival clause if the antecedent is something or someone that is indefinite, negative, vague, or nonexistent.

M.) after **por más que** *or* **por mucho que**.

N.) after the expression **ojalá (que),** *which expresses a great desire.*

THIS PAGE IS INTENTIONALLY BLANK.

IMPERFECT SUBJUNCTIVE USAGE CARDS

A.) This past tense is used for the same reasons as the present subjunctive.

B.) The main difference between the present and imperfect subjunctive is the time of the action.

C.) If the verb in the main clause is in the imperfect, preterit, conditional, or past perfect tense, the imperfect subjunctive is ordinarily used in the dependent clause (if use of the subjunctive is required).

D.) The imperfect subjunctive is used after **como si** *to express a condition contrary to fact.*

THIS PAGE IS INTENTIONALLY BLANK.

PRESENT TENSE

(REGULAR –AR VERBS)

SUBJECT PRONOUN	STEM	ENDING	TRANSLATION
1st person singular	________	________	________
2nd person singular	________	________	________
3rd person singular	________	________	________
1st person plural	________	________	________
2nd person plural	________	________	________
3rd person plural	________	________	________

THIS PAGE IS INTENTIONALLY BLANK.

PRESENT TENSE

(REGULAR –ER VERBS)

SUBJECT PRONOUN	STEM	ENDING	TRANSLATION
1st person singular	______	______	______
2nd person singular	______	______	______
3rd person singular	______	______	______
1st person plural	______	______	______
2nd person plural	______	______	______
3rd person plural	______	______	______

THIS PAGE IS INTENTIONALLY BLANK.

PRESENT TENSE

(REGULAR –IR VERBS)

SUBJECT PRONOUN	STEM	ENDING	TRANSLATION
1st person singular	______	______	______
2nd person singular	______	______	______
3rd person singular	______	______	______
1st person plural	______	______	______
2nd person plural	______	______	______
3rd person plural	______	______	______

THIS PAGE IS INTENTIONALLY BLANK.

IMPERFECT TENSE

(REGULAR –AR VERBS)

SUBJECT PRONOUN	STEM	ENDING	TRANSLATION
1st person singular			
2nd person singular			
3rd person singular			
1st person plural			
2nd person plural			
3rd person plural			

THIS PAGE IS INTENTIONALLY BLANK.

IMPERFECT TENSE

(REGULAR –ER VERBS)

SUBJECT PRONOUN	STEM	ENDING	TRANSLATION
1st person singular	______	______	______
2nd person singular	______	______	______
3rd person singular	______	______	______
1st person plural	______	______	______
2nd person plural	______	______	______
3rd person plural	______	______	______

THIS PAGE IS INTENTIONALLY BLANK.

IMPERFECT TENSE

(REGULAR –IR VERBS)

SUBJECT PRONOUN	STEM	ENDING	TRANSLATION
1st person singular	______	______	______
2nd person singular	______	______	______
3rd person singular	______	______	______
1st person plural	______	______	______
2nd person plural	______	______	______
3rd person plural	______	______	______

THIS PAGE IS INTENTIONALLY BLANK.

PRETERIT TENSE

(REGULAR –AR VERBS)

SUBJECT PRONOUN	STEM	ENDING	TRANSLATION
1st person singular	______	______	______
2nd person singular	______	______	______
3rd person singular	______	______	______
1st person plural	______	______	______
2nd person plural	______	______	______
3rd person plural	______	______	______

THIS PAGE IS INTENTIONALLY BLANK.

PRETERIT TENSE

(REGULAR –ER VERBS)

SUBJECT PRONOUN	STEM	ENDING	TRANSLATION
1st person singular	__________	__________	__________
2nd person singular	__________	__________	__________
3rd person singular	__________	__________	__________
1st person plural	__________	__________	__________
2nd person plural	__________	__________	__________
3rd person plural	__________	__________	__________

THIS PAGE IS INTENTIONALLY BLANK.

PRETERIT TENSE

(REGULAR –IR VERBS)

SUBJECT PRONOUN	STEM	ENDING	TRANSLATION
1st person singular	______	______	______
2nd person singular	______	______	______
3rd person singular	______	______	______
1st person plural	______	______	______
2nd person plural	______	______	______
3rd person plural	______	______	______

THIS PAGE IS INTENTIONALLY BLANK.

FUTURE TENSE

(REGULAR –AR VERBS)

SUBJECT PRONOUN	STEM	ENDING	TRANSLATION
1st person singular	____________	____________	____________
2nd person singular	____________	____________	____________
3rd person singular	____________	____________	____________
1st person plural	____________	____________	____________
2nd person plural	____________	____________	____________
3rd person plural	____________	____________	____________

THIS PAGE IS INTENTIONALLY BLANK.

FUTURE TENSE

(REGULAR –ER VERBS)

SUBJECT PRONOUN	STEM	ENDING	TRANSLATION
1st person singular	________________	________________	________________
2nd person singular	________________	________________	________________
3rd person singular	________________	________________	________________
1st person plural	________________	________________	________________
2nd person plural	________________	________________	________________
3rd person plural	________________	________________	________________

THIS PAGE IS INTENTIONALLY BLANK.

FUTURE TENSE

(REGULAR –IR VERBS)

SUBJECT PRONOUN	STEM	ENDING	TRANSLATION
1st person singular	______	______	______
2nd person singular	______	______	______
3rd person singular	______	______	______
1st person plural	______	______	______
2nd person plural	______	______	______
3rd person plural	______	______	______

THIS PAGE IS INTENTIONALLY BLANK.

CONDITIONAL TENSE

(REGULAR –AR VERBS)

SUBJECT PRONOUN	STEM	ENDING	TRANSLATION
1st person singular	______	______	______
2nd person singular	______	______	______
3rd person singular	______	______	______
1st person plural	______	______	______
2nd person plural	______	______	______
3rd person plural	______	______	______

THIS PAGE IS INTENTIONALLY BLANK.

CONDITIONAL TENSE

(REGULAR –ER VERBS)

SUBJECT PRONOUN	STEM	ENDING	TRANSLATION
1st person singular	______	______	______
2nd person singular	______	______	______
3rd person singular	______	______	______
1st person plural	______	______	______
2nd person plural	______	______	______
3rd person plural	______	______	______

THIS PAGE IS INTENTIONALLY BLANK.

CONDITIONAL TENSE

(REGULAR –IR VERBS)

SUBJECT PRONOUN	STEM	ENDING	TRANSLATION
1st person singular	____________	____________	____________
2nd person singular	____________	____________	____________
3rd person singular	____________	____________	____________
1st person plural	____________	____________	____________
2nd person plural	____________	____________	____________
3rd person plural	____________	____________	____________

THIS PAGE IS INTENTIONALLY BLANK.

PRESENT SUBJUNCTIVE

(REGULAR –AR VERBS)

SUBJECT PRONOUN	STEM	ENDING	TRANSLATION
1st person singular	____________	____________	____________
2nd person singular	____________	____________	____________
3rd person singular	____________	____________	____________
1st person plural	____________	____________	____________
2nd person plural	____________	____________	____________
3rd person plural	____________	____________	____________

THIS PAGE IS INTENTIONALLY BLANK.

PRESENT SUBJUNCTIVE

(REGULAR –ER VERBS)

SUBJECT PRONOUN	STEM	ENDING	TRANSLATION
1st person singular	______	______	______
2nd person singular	______	______	______
3rd person singular	______	______	______
1st person plural	______	______	______
2nd person plural	______	______	______
3rd person plural	______	______	______

THIS PAGE IS INTENTIONALLY BLANK.

PRESENT SUBJUNCTIVE

(REGULAR –IR VERBS)

SUBJECT PRONOUN	STEM	ENDING	TRANSLATION
1st person singular	__________	__________	__________
2nd person singular	__________	__________	__________
3rd person singular	__________	__________	__________
1st person plural	__________	__________	__________
2nd person plural	__________	__________	__________
3rd person plural	__________	__________	__________

THIS PAGE IS INTENTIONALLY BLANK.

IMPERFECT SUBJUNCTIVE

(REGULAR –AR VERBS)

SUBJECT PRONOUN	STEM	ENDING	TRANSLATION
1st person singular	____________	____________	____________
2nd person singular	____________	____________	____________
3rd person singular	____________	____________	____________
1st person plural	____________	____________	____________
2nd person plural	____________	____________	____________
3rd person plural	____________	____________	____________

THIS PAGE IS INTENTIONALLY BLANK.

IMPERFECT SUBJUNCTIVE

(REGULAR –ER VERBS)

SUBJECT PRONOUN	STEM	ENDING	TRANSLATION
1st person singular	__________	__________	__________
2nd person singular	__________	__________	__________
3rd person singular	__________	__________	__________
1st person plural	__________	__________	__________
2nd person plural	__________	__________	__________
3rd person plural	__________	__________	__________

THIS PAGE IS INTENTIONALLY BLANK.

IMPERFECT SUBJUNCTIVE

(REGULAR –IR VERBS)

SUBJECT PRONOUN	STEM	ENDING	TRANSLATION
1st person singular	________	________	________
2nd person singular	________	________	________
3rd person singular	________	________	________
1st person plural	________	________	________
2nd person plural	________	________	________
3rd person plural	________	________	________

THIS PAGE IS INTENTIONALLY BLANK.

SUBJECT PRONOUNS

PRESENT	IMPERFECT	PRETERIT	FUTURE	CONDITIONAL	PRESENT SUBJUNCTIVE	IMPERFECT SUBJUNCTIVE
Yo	Yo	Yo	Yo	Yo	Yo	Yo
Tú	Tú	Tú	Tú	Tú	Tú	Tú
El Ella	El Ella	El Ella	El Ella	El Ella	El Ella	El Ella
Nosotros Nosotras	Nosotros Nosotras	Nosotros Nosotras	Nosotros Nosotras	Nosotros Nosotras	Nosotros Nosotras	Nosotros Nosotras
Vosotros Vosotras	Vosotros Vosotras	Vosotros Vosotras	Vosotros Vosotras	Vosotros Vosotras	Vosotros Vosotras	Vosotros Vosotras
Ellos Ellas	Ellos Ellas	Ellos Ellas	Ellos Ellas	Ellos Ellas	Ellos Ellas	Ellos Ellas

THIS PAGE IS INTENTIONALLY BLANK.

VERB STEM (HABLAR)

PRESENT	IMPERFECT	PRETERIT	FUTURE	CONDITIONAL	PRESENT SUBJUNCTIVE	IMPERFECT SUBJUNCTIVE
habl-	**habl-**	**habl-**	**hablar-**	**hablar-**	**habl-**	**habl-**
habl-	**habl-**	**habl-**	**hablar-**	**hablar-**	**habl-**	**habl-**
habl-	**habl-**	**habl-**	**hablar-**	**hablar-**	**habl-**	**habl-**
habl-	**habl-**	**habl-**	**hablar-**	**hablar-**	**habl-**	**habl-**
habl-	**habl-**	**habl-**	**hablar-**	**hablar-**	**habl-**	**habl-**
habl-	**habl-**	**habl-**	**hablar-**	**hablar-**	**habl-**	**habl-**

THIS PAGE IS INTENTIONALLY BLANK.

VERB ENDINGS (REGULAR –AR)

PRESENT	IMPERFECT	PRETERIT	FUTURE	CONDITIONAL	PRESENT SUBJUNCTIVE	IMPERFECT SUBJUNCTIVE
o	aba	é	é	ía	e	ara
as	abas	aste	ás	ías	es	aras
a	aba	ó	á	ía	e	ara
amos	ábamos	amos	emos	íamos	emos	áramos
áis	abais	asteis	éis	íais	éis	arais
an	aban	aron	án	ían	en	aran

THIS PAGE IS INTENTIONALLY BLANK.

TRANSLATIONS (HABLAR)

PRESENT	IMPERFECT	PRETERIT	FUTURE	CONDITIONAL	PRESENT SUBJUNCTIVE	IMPERFECT SUBJUNCTIVE
I speak	**I was speaking**	**I spoke**	**I shall speak**	**I would speak**	**That I may speak**	**That I might speak**
You speak	**You were speaking**	**You spoke**	**You will speak**	**You would speak**	**That you may speak**	**That you might speak**
He / She speaks	**He / She was speaking**	**He / She spoke**	**He / She will speak**	**He / She would speak**	**That he / she may speak**	**That he / she might speak**
We speak	**We were speaking**	**We spoke**	**We shall speak**	**We would speak**	**That we may speak**	**That we might speak**
You (plural) speak	**You (plural) were speaking**	**You (plural) spoke**	**You (plural) will speak**	**You (plural) would speak**	**That you (plural) may speak**	**That you (plural) might speak**
They speak	**They were speaking**	**They spoke**	**They will speak**	**They would speak**	**That they may speak**	**That they might speak**

THIS PAGE IS INTENTIONALLY BLANK.

SUBJECT PRONOUNS

PRESENT	IMPERFECT	PRETERIT	FUTURE	CONDITIONAL	PRESENT SUBJUNCTIVE	IMPERFECT SUBJUNCTIVE
Yo	**Yo**	**Yo**	**Yo**	**Yo**	**Yo**	**Yo**
Tú	**Tú**	**Tú**	**Tú**	**Tú**	**Tú**	**Tú**
El **Ella**	**El** **Ella**	**El** **Ella**	**El** **Ella**	**El** **Ella**	**El** **Ella**	**El** **Ella**
Nosotros **Nosotras**	**Nosotros** **Nosotras**	**Nosotros** **Nosotras**	**Nosotros** **Nosotras**	**Nosotros** **Nosotras**	**Nosotros** **Nosotras**	**Nosotros** **Nosotras**
Vosotros **Vosotras**	**Vosotros** **Vosotras**	**Vosotros** **Vosotras**	**Vosotros** **Vosotras**	**Vosotros** **Vosotras**	**Vosotros** **Vosotras**	**Vosotros** **Vosotras**
Ellos **Ellas**	**Ellos** **Ellas**	**Ellos** **Ellas**	**Ellos** **Ellas**	**Ellos** **Ellas**	**Ellos** **Ellas**	**Ellos** **Ellas**

THIS PAGE IS INTENTIONALLY BLANK.

VERB STEM (COMER)

PRESENT	IMPERFECT	PRETERIT	FUTURE	CONDITIONAL	PRESENT SUBJUNCTIVE	IMPERFECT SUBJUNCTIVE
com-	com-	com-	comer-	comer-	com-	com-
com-	com-	com-	comer-	comer-	com-	com-
com-	com-	com-	comer-	comer-	com-	com-
com-	com-	com-	comer-	comer-	com-	com-
com-	com-	com-	comer-	comer-	com-	com-
com-	com-	com-	comer-	comer-	com-	com-

THIS PAGE IS INTENTIONALLY BLANK.

VERB ENDINGS (REGULAR –ER)

PRESENT	IMPERFECT	PRETERIT	FUTURE	CONDITIONAL	PRESENT SUBJUNCTIVE	IMPERFECT SUBJUNCTIVE
o	**ía**	**í**	**é**	**ía**	**a**	**iera**
es	**ías**	**iste**	**ás**	**ías**	**as**	**ieras**
e	**ía**	**ió**	**á**	**ía**	**a**	**iera**
emos	**íamos**	**imos**	**emos**	**íamos**	**amos**	**iéramos**
éis	**íais**	**isteis**	**éis**	**íais**	**áis**	**ierais**
en	**ían**	**ieron**	**án**	**ían**	**an**	**ieran**

THIS PAGE IS INTENTIONALLY BLANK.

TRANSLATIONS (COMER)

PRESENT	IMPERFECT	PRETERIT	FUTURE	CONDITIONAL	PRESENT SUBJUNCTIVE	IMPERFECT SUBJUNCTIVE
I **eat**	**I** **was eating**	**I** **ate**	**I** **shall eat**	**I** **would eat**	**That I** **may eat**	**That I** **might eat**
You **eat**	**You** **were eating**	**You** **ate**	**You** **will eat**	**You** **would eat**	**That you** **may eat**	**That you** **might eat**
He / She **eats**	**He / She** **was eating**	**He / She** **ate**	**He / She** **will eat**	**He / She** **would eat**	**That he / she** **may eat**	**That he / she** **might eat**
We **eat**	**We** **were eating**	**We** **ate**	**We** **shall eat**	**We** **would eat**	**That we** **may eat**	**That we** **might eat**
You (plural) **eat**	**You (plural)** **were eating**	**You (plural)** **ate**	**You (plural)** **will eat**	**You (plural)** **would eat**	**That you (plural)** **may eat**	**That you (plural)** **might eat**
They **eat**	**They** **were eating**	**They** **ate**	**They** **will eat**	**They** **would eat**	**That they** **may eat**	**That they** **might eat**

THIS PAGE IS INTENTIONALLY BLANK.

SUBJECT PRONOUNS

PRESENT	IMPERFECT	PRETERIT	FUTURE	CONDITIONAL	PRESENT SUBJUNCTIVE	IMPERFECT SUBJUNCTIVE
Yo	Yo	Yo	Yo	Yo	Yo	Yo
Tú	Tú	Tú	Tú	Tú	Tú	Tú
El Ella	El Ella	El Ella	El Ella	El Ella	El Ella	El Ella
Nosotros Nosotras	Nosotros Nosotras	Nosotros Nosotras	Nosotros Nosotras	Nosotros Nosotras	Nosotros Nosotras	Nosotros Nosotras
Vosotros Vosotras	Vosotros Vosotras	Vosotros Vosotras	Vosotros Vosotras	Vosotros Vosotras	Vosotros Vosotras	Vosotros Vosotras
Ellos Ellas	Ellos Ellas	Ellos Ellas	Ellos Ellas	Ellos Ellas	Ellos Ellas	Ellos Ellas

THIS PAGE IS INTENTIONALLY BLANK.

VERB STEM (VIVIR)

PRESENT	IMPERFECT	PRETERIT	FUTURE	CONDITIONAL	PRESENT SUBJUNCTIVE	IMPERFECT SUBJUNCTIVE
viv-	**viv-**	**viv-**	**vivir-**	**vivir-**	**viv-**	**viv-**
viv-	**viv-**	**viv-**	**vivir-**	**vivir-**	**viv-**	**viv-**
viv-	**viv-**	**viv-**	**vivir-**	**vivir-**	**viv-**	**viv-**
viv-	**viv-**	**viv-**	**vivir-**	**vivir-**	**viv-**	**viv-**
viv-	**viv-**	**viv-**	**vivir-**	**vivir-**	**viv-**	**viv-**
viv-	**viv-**	**viv-**	**vivir-**	**vivir-**	**viv-**	**viv-**

THIS PAGE IS INTENTIONALLY BLANK.

VERB ENDINGS (REGULAR –IR)

PRESENT	IMPERFECT	PRETERIT	FUTURE	CONDITIONAL	PRESENT SUBJUNCTIVE	IMPERFECT SUBJUNCTIVE
o	**ía**	**í**	**é**	**ía**	**a**	**iera**
es	**ías**	**iste**	**ás**	**ías**	**as**	**ieras**
e	**ía**	**ió**	**á**	**ía**	**a**	**iera**
imos	**íamos**	**imos**	**emos**	**íamos**	**amos**	**iéramos**
ís	**íais**	**isteis**	**éis**	**íais**	**áis**	**ierais**
en	**ían**	**ieron**	**án**	**ían**	**an**	**ieran**

THIS PAGE IS INTENTIONALLY BLANK.

TRANSLATIONS (VIVIR)

PRESENT	IMPERFECT	PRETERIT	FUTURE	CONDITIONAL	PRESENT SUBJUNCTIVE	IMPERFECT SUBJUNCTIVE
I live	**I was living**	**I lived**	**I shall live**	**I would live**	**That I may live**	**That I might live**
You live	**You were living**	**You lived**	**You will live**	**You would live**	**That you may live**	**That you might live**
He / She lives	**He / She was living**	**He / She lived**	**He / She will live**	**He / She would live**	**That he / she may live**	**That he / she might live**
We live	**We were living**	**We lived**	**We shall live**	**We would live**	**That we may live**	**That we might live**
You (plural) live	**You (plural) were living**	**You (plural) lived**	**You (plural) will live**	**You (plural) would live**	**That you (plural) may live**	**That you (plural) might live**
They live	**They were living**	**They lived**	**They will live**	**They would live**	**That they may live**	**That they might live**

Printed in the United States
131975LV00015B/22/P

9 781435 704206